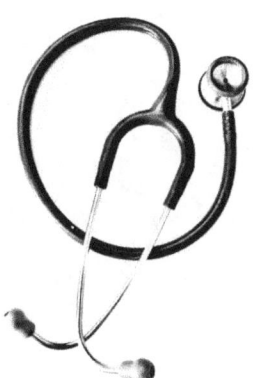

Your Kind of Meditation Series

MEDITATION FOR NURSES

From Beeps to Breaths:
A Practical Guide to Meditation and Mindfulness for Nurses

Written by:
K.J. Stewart

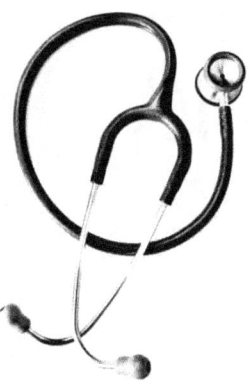

...for every Nurse, everywhere

Table of Contents

Introduction

Shift Happens.

Let's face it; nursing is a lot like being on a roller-coaster. One minute you're a Superhero saving lives, the next you're trying to figure out how to untangle a patient's IV, in a dark room without waking them up.

In the midst of all this chaos, finding peace might feel like trying to find a quiet moment at a rock concert. But fear not, fellow healthcare heroes! Meditation is here to save the day (or at least your sanity).

This book is your go-to guide for incorporating mindfulness and meditation into your hectic nursing life. You might be thinking, "I don't have time for anything like this at work!" Okay, fair enough. That may be the way you feel now and it's totally understandable.

However, if you give the teachings in this book an honest try, you'll find that you do have time. It's simply a matter of knowing how to, when to and acting on what you know.

We'll explore the benefits of mindfulness and meditation, from reducing stress to improving your bedside manner (even when dealing with that one patient who insists on using the call button as a servant's bell).

We'll also dive into practical techniques, from quick mindfulness exercises geared for work to longer, more immersive meditations that can be practiced at home or in nature.

While this information will help you incorporate meditation into your life, it's important to note that none of these techniques should ever be practiced in a way, or at a time that endangers yourself or a patient in your care.

Several of the techniques found in this book are repeated within the examples of different work situations. The hope is that you will find one that "sounds do-able" and actually try it.

These meditation and mindfulness techniques really work and are not hard to learn at all. So, grab your favorite comfy chair, a cup of tea (or preferred liquid) and let's embark on a journey toward a more peaceful, mindful, and less chaotic nursing career.

Chapter One

The Importance of Meditation

The Nurse Superhero Quiz

Does this sound like you?

- Your coffee mug holds a mystery concoction that fuels your epic 12-hour shift and possesses near-magical stimulating properties.

- You've perfected the "comfort squeeze" – a gentle shoulder pat that speaks volumes: empathy, reassurance, and silent support.

- You can translate complex medical jargon into terms that would make it easy for a toddler to understand, all while maintaining a professional smile.

- You're a problem fixer, a negotiator and to those you care for, an Angel in uniform.

- You anticipate a patient's needs before they even hit the call button – you're practically a mind-reader in scrubs!

- You do all of this at times with very little help and very little sleep.

- And yes, there are those who have even more to do once they get home. Superhero Nurse turns into Superhero Mom, Dad, wife or husband.

If this sounds like you, then congratulations. You, my friend, are a certified Nurse Superhero. Consider this book the user manual for accessing your Superpower. Now, let's add some real peace to your arsenal of survival!

Why Meditation Matters for Nurses

Nurses are the backbone of the healthcare system. You navigate complex medical situations, provide emotional support to patients and their families, and advocate for their well-being. Did we mention trying to have a home life too?

You are the center point of family concern and patient worry. You take it all on, because it's what you do as a Nurse.

It's no surprise that this demanding work can take a toll and seem to drain the soul. Long hours, emotional intensity, and constant pressure can lead to stress, burnout, and compassion fatigue.

Meditation can be your secret weapon to combat these challenges and emerge as a stronger, more peaceful and centered nurse.

Finding peace and balance in your life might not seem possible right now, but don't believe that illusion.

Peace is not only possible; it is your very nature. The following pages will show you how to verify that statement as truth in your own life through mindfulness and meditation.

Chapter Two

Understanding Meditation

What Meditation is Not:
Ditch the Incense, Embrace the Fuzzy Socks

Alright, white coat warriors! You've heard the whispers – meditation, the secret weapon for inner peace and stress-slaying.

But before you picture yourself levitating in a cloud of incense smoke while chanting something vaguely Sanskrit-sounding, let's debunk some myths and get you on the path to peace, nurse-style.

Myth #1 You Need Full Lotus Pose and Flowy Robes

Newsflash: meditation isn't a pretzel contest. Sitting comfortably is key, but comfort can come in many forms.

Think comfy chair, couch potato position, even a pile of pillows on the floor (just don't fall asleep!).

Flowy robes are great for fantasy novels, but real nurses know the power of a good pair of comfy socks. Sit relaxed, comfortable and simply breathe.

Myth #2 It's About Emptying Your Mind

Let's be honest, an empty mind for a nurse is a recipe for disaster (have you ever forgotten a medication?).

Meditation is more about acknowledging your thoughts, like pesky little squirrels in your brain forest.

You don't need to banish them, just observe them without judgment and gently guide your attention back to your breath when it wanders. There's no need to engage with every squirrel that runs by, just observe and breathe.

Myth #3 It Takes Hours and Hours

Even Florence Nightingale needed a break! Meditation can be as short as 1 to 5 minutes. Think of it as a mental mini-vacation. A few precious moments of quiet can make a world of difference in your day.

You can become mindful of your breath while walking down the hall to a patient, when you get supplies or when you take a break.

You're only looking for a couple of minutes to observe your breath and allow the mind to calm.

So, What Actually *Is* Meditation?

Being a nurse can sometimes feel like a real whirlwind. Meditation isn't about forcing control over that whirlwind, but rather, finding a pocket of quiet within it.

While a quick break to "grab a drink" or "pee" can offer temporary relief, meditation is a proactive approach to manage stress and cultivate inner strength - peace.

Imagine it as an investment in your well-being, just like getting enough sleep or eating healthy meals.

The benefits of this practice extend far beyond the immediate quiet time. Mindfulness and meditation are often used interchangeably, but they have distinct meanings.

Mindfulness is a state of being fully present and aware of your thoughts, feelings, and surroundings without judgment. It's a way of living in the present moment.

Meditation is a specific practice that can help cultivate mindfulness. It's a practice that helps you realize your true peaceful nature, prior to the activity of a busy mind.

While meditation is a common way to practice mindfulness, it's not the only way. You can also be mindful while going for a walk, eating a meal, or even during a stressful situation at work.

In essence, Mindfulness is the destination, a state of being present and aware. Meditation is the vehicle, a practice that helps you reach that destination.

While this concept of a destination is helpful for understanding the experience, you really don't "go" anywhere to reach your peace. It's already right there within you.

Here is a core example of the kinds of techniques you'll be offered in this book. Imagine the rush of a busy shift. You've got a great many things on your mind and more incoming. You have charting to do and a staff meeting in 20 minutes.

Now, PAUSE, focus your attention on your breath, the rise and fall of your chest as the air moves in and out.

As your attention settles with each inhale and exhale, a sense of calm emerges, a mini-refuge in the storm. It's that simple. The hard part it seems, is remembering to Pause and do it.

With each practice, this peaceful awareness deepens and becomes easier to access. It becomes a wonderful balancing tool for your life and the incredible work you do.

With even a modest effort, meditating will help you develop the ability to access the peace within yourself, to withdraw from thoughts and rest in a silent awareness within – you know it as a deep feeling of peace. Though some may laugh at the idea of meditation, it's no joke.

It's important to remember that, no one who has truly practiced these techniques has ever failed to reduce chaos and stress in their life. No one!

Remember, "knowing the techniques" and actually "doing them" are two very different things. Make a little time for this, because you are worth the effort.

Chapter Three

Understanding the Impact of Stress on Nurses

(Stuff you probably already know)

Physiological Effects: Chronic stress manifests in physical ways. It can weaken your immune system, making you more susceptible to illness.

Elevated stress hormones can contribute to headaches, muscle tension, and digestive issues. These physical ailments can impact your ability to perform your duties effectively.

Emotional Effects: Stress can drain your emotional reserves, leading to feelings of irritability, anxiety, and even depression.

This negativity can spill over into your interactions with patients and colleagues, hindering communication and creating a tense work environment.

Compassion Fatigue: Witnessing suffering every day can take an emotional toll. Compassion fatigue makes it difficult to maintain empathy and offer emotional support to your patients. Meditation can help build resilience against this emotional exhaustion.

The Downward Daily Spiral and how to change it

Ah, nurses. The Superheroes of the medical world, saving lives and juggling chaos with the grace of a ballerina on a tightrope.

But even the most dedicated heroes have their kryptonite, and for nurses, that kryptonite often arrives in the form of being short staffed or the feeling of a never-ending shift.

Many nurses don't realize they are going down the stress road until they find themselves in Pain Town or Fatigue City (we don't recommend either – awful hospitality).

Sometimes, you can get so used to it, stress can seem like the normal routine, but it's not. Realizing you are stressed is the first step away from it.

Next, let's talk about the spiraling path many Nurses find themselves on and the techniques for turning it around.

The "Daily Downward Spiral of the Stressed Nurse" paints a picture more harrowing than sailing through a hurricane in a leaky rowboat.

But fear not, there's a way to escape this nightmarish cycle and emerge victorious: **Meditation.**

You don't need to learn all of the techniques found in this book, just find one to practice. That's really all it takes to break the spiral. Again, if something you read resonates with you, sounds good or feels appropriate, give it a try.

Breaking the Daily Spiral

Here are a few snapshots of the daily spiral and the techniques for turning each around and finding balance.

The Caffeinated Crusader

Our story begins with our intrepid nurse, breezing into their shift with a smile and a thermos of coffee that could wake the dead (or at least get them talking about their grandchildren).

Charts are conquered, medications dispensed, and patients soothed with the gentle efficiency of a well-oiled machine. Repeated day after day, the reliance on coffee grows.

To keep this in check, you can use meditation to balance caffeine consumption. We're not talking about eliminating coffee, not at all.

Instead, we are suggesting using meditation as a source of energy and for the same reasons you drink coffee.

Including a brief mindfulness practice in your morning routine can manifest a deep sense of peace to go with your wonderful cup of coffee.

Such a practice can help you decrease the amount of caffeine and maintain the same energy level.

This happens naturally when you're reducing stress and sleeping better.

Once you find your balance, coffee becomes something you drink only when you want to, no longer because you feel you have to.

Yes, there will always be the occasional two cup days, however, the habitual reliance on it for daily energy is far less or eliminated totally.

The Beleaguered Battler

As the hours of the shift tick by, the tide begins to turn. The ever-present call light symphony intensifies. The once-crisp uniform now bears the faint insignia of a rogue droplet of who-knows-what.

The smile? Strained, but still there. Coffee? Now a lukewarm, questionable concoction best described as "life juice." A quick glance at the time, followed by the thought "how many hours are left?"

As the day moves on, you're faced with constant interruptions, workload build up and information overload. The mind can feel overwhelmed and prioritizing can sometimes become difficult.

It's at this point you can use a short 1 minute meditation to calm the mind, bring about clarity and focus on priorities. It truly grounds you in peace, which changes the way you experience the moment.

It will make a world of difference and no one will even know that you're doing it. When the moment comes, PAUSE, with your eyes open, shift your attention to your chest or stomach.

Simply remain aware of your body breathing, the rise and fall of your chest as the air moves in and out. That's all.

You'll look as if you're thinking, but in fact the experience is quite the opposite. Thoughts are calming and peace is asserting itself.

After about a minute, take a deep breath and resume what you were doing. This can really settle you and change a moment for the better, especially when practiced daily.

You'll find that each time you practice this; you regain your peace quicker. This small action makes such a huge difference.

As you can see, the instructions are indeed simple and you'll find even more examples in the following pages.

When you give it a try, you'll find that taking just 1 or 2 minutes to become mindful will enhance focus, improve your decision-making and increase productivity. More peace is truly experienced in every aspect of your life.

It's amazing how much of a positive impact just a couple of minutes of mindful breathing can have on a moment, a day or a lifetime.

The Frazzled Flash

The shift deepens, and our hero transforms into a whirlwind of activity. Eyes darting, clipboard clutched white-knuckled, muttering about "where are those freaking IV poles?!"

The smile? A distant memory, replaced by a determined grimace. The coffee? Gone, replaced by a desperate swig from a (hopefully yours) water bottle.

By now, you're running on fumes and adrenaline. Nerves are on edge and you're on an emotional roller coaster ride. Every Doctor seems to have an issue and every patient seems to need you, right now.

This is where a regular meditation practice really helps. If you find yourself in this predicament, then some mindful breathing will help you greatly in that moment.

However, with a daily meditation practice, you develop the ability to witness emotion, but not become it. You're less swept away by emotion.

With practice, you'll find yourself in those stressful situations less often. But when you do, you'll have the ability to change the way you're experiencing it. Same situation, a lot less stress.

The end result of a consistent meditation routine, even a short one, is improved stress management, increased patience, more peace and better sleep.

The Sleep-Deprived Samurai

The night shift passes. Dawn approaches, painting the sky with streaks of hope (and exhaustion). Our hero, now a sleep-deprived samurai, fights a losing battle against the urge to doze off mid-sentence.

Hallucinations of missing charts and talking stethoscopes are just around the corner. The once-proud uniform resembles a war-torn flag. Coffee? A distant dream.

We are talking about chronic sleep deprivation. It doesn't matter if you're working the day shift or the night, trying to perform your job with little sleep is extremely difficult and can be dangerous.

A regular meditation routine will improve the quality of rest and sleep while at home. It helps you rest your body and your mind, making the way for a deeper sleep. A more restful night makes for a smoother day.

With a regular meditation practice (even a short one), you'll find clarity, reduced stress and an enhanced mood. All of which contribute to a more restful and deep sleep. No need to count sheep, just observe your breath.

The Post-Shift Slump

I'm home! Finally, sweet release! The shift ends, and our hero collapses into a chair, transformed into a deflated balloon animal. Sleep beckons, a sirens song promising oblivion.

"Sleepy eating" takes over as you munch your way to the bedroom. Do I shower or not? Was there something I was supposed to do?

Little decisions become difficult. You finally lay down and are either asleep as soon as your head hits the pillow or you lay there thinking until you pass out. You gave this day all you could.

But rest assured, dear nurse, tomorrow is a new day, and with a fresh pot of coffee, you'll rise again, ready to battle the ever-present chaos. After all, isn't that the life of a Superhero Nurse, stressed and often sleep-deprived?

Perhaps it is now, BUT, it doesn't have to be. Turn it around and break the spiral using meditation. If you develop a daily meditation practice, even a short one, you'll find yourself changing (not like the incredible hulk), but in a wonderful way.

The post shift slump turns into a more healthy stress free routine, followed by deep restful sleep. The experience of feeling beaten or drained fades.

You begin to balance every aspect of your life through a simple short meditation. The stress that once held you down loses its grip on you – all because you meditated. Now, let's look at some of the benefits of meditation beyond those already mentioned.

Chapter Four

How Meditation Benefits Nurses

Stress Reduction: Meditation promotes relaxation by quieting the mind (allowing it to calm) and focusing on the present moment. You pause to become aware of your own breathing.

By consciously settling your breath and observing your thoughts without judgment, you learn to detach from the constant mental chatter that fuels anxiety. By focusing attention on your breathing, you withdraw it from the activity of thought (mind). This allows your body and mind to enter a state of deep rest, even in short bursts.

Enhanced Focus and Clarity: Regular meditation practice improves your ability to concentrate and maintain focus under pressure. This translates to sharper decision-making at the bedside and better information processing during critical situations.

Emotional Regulation: Through meditation, you develop the skill to observe your emotions without getting swept away by them.

This allows you to respond calmly and effectively to challenging situations instead of reacting out of stress or frustration.

Increased Self-Compassion: Meditation fosters self-awareness and a sense of self-compassion. You learn to acknowledge your vulnerabilities and limitations without judgment. This allows you to prioritize your own well-being, preventing burnout and promoting self care.

Improved Patient Care: When you operate from a place of calm and centeredness, your interactions with patients become more compassionate and effective.

You have the emotional space to listen attentively, offer genuine support, and create a healing environment.

You've become this still, peaceful presence because you have been practicing mindfulness and meditation.

You learn to stand on the banks of the emotional river and watch it go by, attentive, yet unattached. You still experience emotion, but it doesn't take you over because you're anchored in peace. Now let's look at a few reasons to practice mindfulness as a Nurse.

Meditation for the Weary Nurse

Alright, you've battled bodily fluids of questionable origin, soothed existential dread with a spoonful of sugar coated wisdom and navigated the bureaucratic labyrinth like a pro.

But even the mightiest Nurse needs to take care of their self and find balance in life. That's where meditation comes in – not some woo-woo chanting circle (although, if that's your jam, more power to you!).

Think of it as mental floss for your brain. It's a wonderful way to quickly remove the residual build up of daily activity.

We're talking one to five minutes of quiet – yes, five whole minutes to slay the stress dragon and find inner peace. Don't worry, you won't sprout crystals or levitate (unless you've been exposed to something funky in isolation).

Picture this: a world where the never-ending beeps of the call light symphony don't sound like a horror movie soundtrack. Imagine facing a code blue with the laser focus of a brain surgeon operating on a gnat, not a tired jittery mess fueled by lukewarm cafeteria coffee.

This peace, my friend, is within your reach. It's called meditation, and it's your secret weapon against the stress monster lurking in the hospital corridors.

We've all been there. Drowning in paperwork, short staffed, dodging emotional landmines disguised as patients, and feeling like a hamster stuck on a stress wheel that never stops spinning.

But here's the good news, you can break free from this hamster wheel of doom. Meditation isn't some mystical hocus pocus reserved for yogis contorted into human pretzels.

It's about learning to quiet the mental chatter that sounds like a bunch of squawking parrots arguing over a meal. Just a few minutes a day can work wonders, like a mini mental vacation to the beach where your only worry is which seashell to pick up.

Look at it as a mental reboot. It's a chance to hit the pause button on the chaos and reconnect with the peace that lies within you. By practicing meditation, you're learning how to access that peace and bring more of it into your life.

Throughout this book, you will be given simple techniques, that when earnestly practiced (even a little bit), will yield wonderful and consistent results.

It's not about achieving enlightenment (although that would be pretty cool), it's about learning to observe your thoughts and emotions without getting tangled up in them.

Instead of reacting to a demanding patient like a cat startled by a cucumber, you'll respond with the calm competence of a seasoned nurse who's seen it all (and probably some things you wouldn't believe).

The benefits are real, and they're pretty spectacular. Science, that stuffy guy in a lab coat, says meditation reduces stress hormones faster than a cold shower, improves focus and helps you manage your emotions better than a therapist with a lifetime supply of tissues.

You'll sleep so much better, be more present with your patients (because let's face it, sometimes we're all on autopilot), and rediscover the joy of doing what you do for a living. All of this is only a breath away. Literally!

Don't let the fancy word "meditation" scare you off. It's easier than you might think. Start with one to five minutes a day, focusing on your breath.

Feel your belly rise and fall. Observe the body breathing. That's it! Focus your attention on the air moving in and out with each inhale and exhale.

If your mind wanders off to that time you accidentally called Dr. Johnson "Dr. Doolittle," gently bring attention back to the breath. That's it! Simple, right?

Simple, yes, but not easy. That's why there are so many examples of how to practice this simple technique in the following pages.

This isn't a magic trick that will make your stress disappear with a puff of smoke (although that would be amazing too).

But it is a powerful tool that can help you reclaim your inner peace and become the superstar nurse you were always meant to be - not just for your patients, but for yourself.

So take a deep breath and embark on this journey to a calmer, less stressed you. You deserve a break from the hospital drama, and meditation is your backstage pass to serenity.

It'll help you develop the ability to witness emotion and not become the emotion, to acknowledge stress, but not become lost in it. Your actions become conscious actions instead of emotional reactions.

This is about becoming a calmer, sharper version of your already-amazing self. This is what meditation does.

This Book Won't Make You Weird – It's just some help Chilling Out

Let's get one thing straight right off the bat; this book isn't here to turn you into a yoga-pretzel-contorting, kale-smoothie-sipping, essential-oil-diffusing caricature of Zen.

If you're picturing mandatory meditation time and group kumbaya sessions, well, you can take a deep breath and release that worry. You will determine when and where you meditate and for how long. This book explains how, whether it's for 2 minutes or 2 hours.

We all know the reality of nursing life, the good and the bad. It's often a whirlwind of beeps, charts, meds, Docs, patients and enough caffeine to fuel a small rocket. We truly understand.

Whether you're looking for just a little help unwinding, or you're desperate to find some peace in your life, the techniques in this book can help.

We're not here to dismantle your entire life and replace it with incense and affirmations. Instead, think of this as your personal handbook for carving out a tiny oasis of calm in the beautiful chaos of nursing.

With practice, you'll realize yourself as the lighthouse in any storm. We'll equip you with tools and tips to quiet the mental chatter, de-stress after a monster shift, and face the next challenge with a smile (or at least a non-gritted-teeth grimace).

As you read on, you'll see how taking just one to five minutes a day for meditation offers a powerful tool to combat the stress spiral.

It's not about achieving nirvana (though that would be nice), but rather learning to quiet the mind, or rather allow the mind to quiet and cultivate peace.

Conquering Chaos with Calm

Let's face it, nurses. Hospitals can be a pressure cooker, and sometimes that coffee just isn't cutting it. But don't worry; we've got some easy breathing techniques that are faster than a code blue and smoother than a freshly made bed (okay, maybe not that smooth).

You know the value of meditation now and you've probably been reminded of your own situation to some degree.

Look, right now you may feel like this is just one more thing I'd have to add to my "to do" list. That's understandable, but you if you give ANY of the techniques found in this book, an honest try, you will not fail to find more peace.

You'll actually find that multi-tasking becomes easier because there is more space between thoughts and choices are made from a place of clarity. With consistent effort, you'll find you embrace life differently.

You really won't experience the activity of life in the same way. You will find more space between your thoughts and actions - not in time, but rather in experience.

You'll feel like you can breathe again, not so over-whelmed, a bit more like a weight has been lifted. This peace and relief is just a breath away.

Pay attention to your "gut" on this. If you feel like one of the mindfulness or meditative techniques in this book sounds good, or you imagine one of them might work for you, do it.

You can plan to do it later, but if a technique strikes a cord with you, put the book down and try it. Right then and there. You'll be glad you did.

Chapter Five

Work Related Techniques

Here are some work related mindfulness and meditative techniques to consider. These are specifically related to some of the situations you may encounter as a nurse.

There are even more techniques offered later in the book. Remember, the techniques found here are just starting points. The key is to find what works best for you and practice regularly.

Even a few minutes of meditation can help you feel calmer, more focused, and ready to conquer the next hour or the next shift! Let's start by addressing one of the most common challenges in Nursing.

Defeating the Pre-Shift Jitters

Ah, the pre-shift jitters. That knot of nervous energy that tightens your stomach and makes you question your ability to face the coming chaos.

But fear not, weary warrior! These meditations will equip you with the tools to vanquish those jitters and step onto the battlefield (hospital floor) with calm resolve.

Remember, there is no need to worry about what others think regarding your meditation. They're not even going to know unless you tell them. This is about YOU and the peace you are.

Pre Shift Prep

The following meditations are excellent for stabilizing and grounding you in real peace. There are even more to choose from later in the book, some short and some longer.

As always, if one of these sounds good to you, try it! That first little step (trying it) is the first step towards reducing stress and changing the way you experience life for the better.

Ok then, as soon as you're ready, find a quiet corner and get ready to dominate those jitters! The following techniques can be practiced before leaving the house, or upon arriving at work. Each of these techniques can be used at different times and for different reasons. Again, it's about finding ONE technique that works for you.

Pre-Shift Breath

3 Minutes to Inner Peace

Let's start with Pre-shift anxiety. You're staring down a mountain of paperwork, a to-do list longer than your arm, and a premonition that today's shift will be particularly lively.

Now is the time to find that quiet corner, even if it's in the bathroom at home, or the supply closet at work (we won't judge – just be safe).

Close your eyes and focus on your breath. Inhale slowly through your nose for a count of five, feeling your belly inflate like a beach ball.

Hold for a second, then exhale slowly through pursed lips for a count of seven, like you're deflating a balloon. Repeat this for one to three minutes.

This simple belly breathing technique activates your body's relaxation response, washing away pre-shift jitters and leaving you feeling centered.

You'll be ready to tackle whatever the day throws your way. If anxiety rears its head again, repeat the technique. It really works, but you don't have to believe us, test it for yourself.

The Superhero Shuffle

*(Visualization, **Humor**, 1 Minute)*

Ok, this is the funny one so get crazy with it. When a problem arises or a challenge presents itself, take a second to imagine yourself transforming into your Nurse Superhero alter ego. Yes, it feels silly, but try it.

Perhaps you can hear theme music playing in the back ground as you begin to visualize yourself transforming. Maybe you have a cape made of bed sheets or a utility belt stocked with syringes and Band-Aids. Really get silly with it.

See yourself floating above the hospital floor, radiating a light of calm confidence. As you descend, take a deep breath and visualize the jitters shrinking, then transforming into harmless butterflies that flutter away.

As you open your eyes, your Superhero outfit becomes invisible, returning your appearance to normal...but you'll know!

This sounds truly ridiculous, but give it a try. You may be wonderfully surprised at the smile you feel inside. Remember, no one knows what you're doing, but you. The more outrageous the outfit, the bigger the smile.

Laughter is the best medicine, (except for actual medicine, which you are, of course, an expert in) and you'll be surprised at how well this works.

Once you've done it once, you can call upon this comical superhero at any time. Actually, just the thought of peaceful silliness is often enough to slow the breath and calm the mind.

Feeling Your Feet

(Present Moment Awareness, 1 Minute)

Whenever things get really busy, Pause, take a moment to sit quietly. Shift your focus to your physical sensations - what you feel, what you smell or what you hear.

Wiggle your toes in your shoes, feel the chair beneath you, and really focus on the feeling of your breath moving in and out.

Notice any sounds around you, like the hum of the lights or distant chatter. Allow them to come and go, just like the breath. You remain the silent witness.

By anchoring yourself in the present moment, you detach from future worries. You're withdrawing attention from the environment and all its "things".

By remaining aware of your breathing, you are relaxing into your peace, the silent refuge within. After a minute or so, relax your inner gaze and return to normal activity.

Waves Of Life On The Beach of Peace

(3 Minutes)

Whether its pre-shift jitters or you just feel the stress of the day creeping up on you, take a minute to settle. Find a place to sit comfortable, any place will do. Bring your attention to your breath. Simply observe the rise and fall of your chest or stomach.

Once your breathing is relaxed, imagine how similar your breath coming in and out is like the waves washing up on the beach. Coming and going, just like the breath. Coming and going, just like the activities of life.

Now, as you observe this, notice something wonderful. YOU are what doesn't come and go. Like the beach, you are the witness of the waves, of movement, of your breath and of life.

You are the stillness upon which all movement takes place. Rest in this background as you remain aware of the body breathing.

Once you're done, you'll be feeling calmer, more centered and ready to take on whatever the day throws your way. Remember, even Superheroes need a moment to recharge before saving the day (or night).

The Restroom Rescue Breath

(Because Sometimes You Need To)

The Situation: You are at your wits end. The call light symphony is reaching operatic heights, your co-worker just called in sick (again!), and you swear you saw a rogue bedpan rolling down the hallway. You feel like you might lose it... for real.

The Rescue Breath: As soon as you're able, excuse yourself to the restroom or an empty room for a "brief emergency" (wink, wink). Take a few deep, cleansing breaths, focusing on the cool air entering your nostrils and the warm air leaving your mouth. Imagine you're inhaling calm and exhaling the chaos.

After a few slow deep breaths, allow your breathing to return to a relaxed and normal pace. You "Paused", you settled and now you're ready to carry on.

Yes, this sounds "froo froo", but what is really going on is you are pulling your attention away from the environment, away from experience and away from your mind.

You are in fact stepping away from the chaos and into the peaceful refuge you have practiced accessing through meditation.

This quick reset refocuses your mind and calms your nerves. You return to the floor feeling like a Superhero who just discovered their secret power: the power of peaceful breathing!

Post-Patient Drain: The Emotions

You just finished dealing with a patient who could rival any movie villain. You're feeling drained and frustrated. This is when you make a simple choice to do the following.

Stand quietly for a moment, placing one hand on your abdomen. Feel your belly rise and fall with each breath.

Notice any emotions that arise – anger, frustration, maybe even a sprinkle of annoyance? Acknowledge them, but don't judge yourself for feeling human. With each exhale, imagine releasing that tension and negativity.

Once again you are pulling attention back from mind and allowing the thoughts and the emotions to come and go, without holding on to them.

This mindful breathing exercise helps you process your emotions in a healthy way, preventing them from boiling over and affecting your next patient interaction. You'll be back to your compassionate self in no time.

Remember, these are just a few simple techniques you can use throughout your shift. They may not make the charts disappear or magically restock the supply closet, but they will equip you with the inner peace and focus to navigate the storm.

Consider these breaths your secret weapons – because a calm and collected nurse is a truly unstoppable force!

By incorporating these short mindfulness exercises throughout your day, you'll cultivate the ability to better manage the emotional demands of nursing.

You'll find yourself approaching each situation with more focus, clarity, and compassion – for both yourself and your patients.

You've seen some basic techniques already; however, the following techniques address more specific aspects of meditation, like distraction, short attention spans or yo-yo mind.

So read on, and when you're ready, grab a comfy seat and prepare to discover the Superhero within – the calm, centered, and yes, maybe even a little bit happier you.

Remember, while you will find different techniques for different situations throughout this book, the key is to find one, just one that works for you.

Just one mindfulness or meditation technique, earnestly practiced, will reshape your world in a wonderful way.

Meditation for the Short Attention Span

Taming the Monkey Mind in Minutes

Feeling like your brain is a pinball machine on overdrive? Don't worry, even a few moments of mindfulness can make a huge difference.

When you spend time meditating, no matter how short or long of a session, you gain momentum. That turns into an ever-present peace that you have constant access to.

Your inner peace is a lighthouse, the safe harbor in any storm. Mindfulness is the key to the lighthouse.

Here are some easy meditation techniques for those with the attention span of a hummingbird:

1. Popcorn Breathing (2 Minutes)

Explanation: Rapid, short breaths can surprisingly help quiet a racing mind. Imagine yourself popping popcorn!

Steps:

1. Find a comfortable position, sitting or standing. Close your eyes (optional).

2. Take a series of short, quick breaths through your nose, like popping popcorn kernels.

3. Breathe out through your mouth with a gentle "whoosh" sound.

4. Repeat steps 2 and 3 for about 30 to 60 seconds, focusing on the sensation of the breath.

5. Gradually slow down your breathing to a normal pace.

2. The Monkey Mind Trick (3 Minutes)

Explanation: Our thoughts are like playful monkeys – always swinging from branch to branch! This technique helps us acknowledge them without getting involved with them.

Steps:

1. Find a quiet spot and get comfortable. Close
    your eyes (optional).

2. Focus on your breath, feeling the rise and fall
    of your chest. Simply be aware of your body
    breathing. Believe me, you don't have to tell
    it to breath, it will do it all by itself. You just
    observe it.

3. Inevitably, your mind will wander – that's
    really okay! That's what mind is, the activity
    of thoughts. You are the one observing
    them. Imagine your thoughts as monkeys
    swinging through a tree. You observe as if
    you were the tree.

4. When you notice a thought, gently
    acknowledge the thought with a mental
    "monkey!" and guide your attention back to
    your breath.

Example: Lets say you just had the thought "This
technique sounds dumb". Acknowledge that
thought, then mentally call it "monkey".

Every thought you witness is just a swinging monkey. It doesn't mean you have to swing with it. Just watch, remain silent and experience more peace.

A thought may come back, sometimes over and over. However, each time the thought returns, it is weaker. Eventually the thought fades.

You can also exchange the "monkey mind" idea for that of "The tree and leaf. You sit and breathe as a tree would, quietly observing thoughts as leaves, first wiggling in the wind of mind, then falling away.

What you are doing is pulling attention back from mind, away from thoughts. You are reseating perception in awareness, becoming the witness of activity, but not a participant.

Don't get discouraged if your mind wanders often – remember, even monkeys get tired eventually!

Bonus Tip: Feeling restless? Tired of counting the tiles on the ceiling? Try counting your breaths to 10, then starting over if you lose track. It's a simple way to keep your mind engaged without getting overwhelmed.

The Charting Crusaders

Conquering Digital Documentation

Calling all digital defenders! We're swapping highlighters for our trusty cursors and upgrading our focus to dominate those digital documentation marathons.

Let's be honest, electronic charting can feel like navigating a digital labyrinth. Sometimes it goes smooth and sometimes it doesn't.

Whether you are familiar with the charting system or still struggling to learn it, charting mindfully will help you become better at it. Being a Mindful Documenter in the digital world is about efficiency and accuracy.

By focusing on each crucial detail, you'll ensure you capture everything you need, avoiding errors and saving yourself precious time (which, let's be honest, is a nurse's most valuable resource).

Becoming a Digital Documentation Dynamo

Silence the Sirens: Those notification sounds and pop-ups are the digital chart monster's siren song, luring you away from mindful documentation. Silence them!

Put your phone on silent, mute the notifications that can be (not the vital ones), and create a focused workspace that minimizes distractions. Here are a few charting ideas for you to consider.

1. **Channel Your Inner X-Ray Vision:** Imagine you have X-ray vision for crucial information. Scan each section of the chart, mentally prioritizing what needs to be documented.

   Is it meds, vitals, allergies? Focus on that specific data, letting go of irrelevant details (like Mr. Jones' cat pictures – adorable, but not medically relevant).

2. **The Mindful Cursor Maneuver:** This isn't about click-happy highlighting. Treat each piece of information with respect. Read it, understand it, and then click to document it

with intention. This will help eliminate second guessing yourself.

3. **Embrace the Edit Button:** Made a digital documentation mistake? No sweat! That's what the edit button is for. Unlike a high-lighter mishap on paper, you can simply fix your error and move on. Stay away from "I'll fix it later" and do it now.

4. **Master the Keyboard Shortcuts:** You know those little keyboard shortcuts hiding in the menu bar? They're your friends! Learn a few to become a documentation speed demon (the good kind, fueled by focus, not caffeine).

Mind-Calming Techniques for the Digital Doc Crusader

Conquering digital documentation requires a sharp mind and a calm spirit. Here are a few techniques to help you stay focused and centered while documenting:

Deep Breathing: Take a few slow, deep breaths before diving into your charting. Breathe in through your nose for a count of four, hold for a count of two, and exhale slowly through your mouth for a count of six. Repeat this a few times to oxygenate your brain and promote relaxation.

Quick Meditation: With your eyes open, focus on your breathing. Notice the rise and fall of your chest as the air moves in and out. In this practice, you are stepping away from experience and into the clarity of stillness. Simply observe any passing thoughts without judgment, remain uninvolved. As always, gently bring your attention back to your breath when your focus wanders. After about a minute, carry on with work.

Mindful Movement: Feeling restless? Take a short walk or do some gentle stretches at your workstation. A little movement can help to clear your head and refocus your energy.

Remember, becoming a Digital Documentation Dynamo takes practice. Be patient, and celebrate those moments of focused charting. Before you know it, you'll be navigating the digital chart labyrinth with the focus of a Master.

How to Stay Chill When Code Blue Betty Crashes the Party

Nurses, we've all been there. You're settling into a peaceful charting rhythm, maybe even humming a happy tune (because that totally happens), when BAM!

The dreaded overhead speaker crackles to life, and a voice, smooth as sandpaper, announces, "Code Blue in Room 37!" Enter Code Blue Betty, the embodiment of hospital chaos.

But fear not, fellow healthcare heroes! This book equips you with the coping mechanisms of a Superhero (minus the cape, because laundry day is a beast).

Why Inner Peace with Code Blue Betty?

Freaking out during a crisis? Not exactly helpful for you, your patient, or your team. Staying calm and focused allows you to think clearly, react effectively, and maybe even maintain a shred of your sanity (seriously, it's a superpower).

Befriending the Present

Remaining anchored in the peace
of the present moment during an emergency

We all have our internal pep talks. When Betty barges in, we can take a deep breath in and on the exhale, whisper a calming mantra like "This too shall pass" or "I Got This!" Bonus points for a Superhero-themed mantra: "Nurse Wonder Woman, activate!"

These and other techniques in this book may seem silly at first; at least until you do them and they start working.

These simple and yes, odd sounding techniques can make a huge positive impact on your work and your life.

Did you notice "life" and "work" are separated in the last sentence? It's because "work" is what you do, NOT what you are. Remembering that will help you maintain balance in your life.

Critical Moment Breathing Techniques

Your Inner Anchor

Feeling your heart do the samba during a code blue? Lost in worry and under the weight of a heavy workload? Breathing techniques are your anchor in the storm.

The following techniques will help pull you out of the heart racing "mind lock" following the code and into the calm and laser focused Superhero you are.

That ocean of peace is within you and dwelling in it for even a couple of minutes before, during or after a shift will center you, revive you and restore you! Here are a couple of techniques that can really change the moment and fill it with calm.

Box Breathing: Inhale for a count of four, hold for four, exhale for four, hold for four. Repeat. Simple, yet powerful.

This technique can completely change a stressful moment. It's also really good for finding clarity in chaos or if you are simply in need of a pre-panic rescue.

4-4-8 Breathing: Breathe in for four seconds, hold for four seconds, exhale slowly for eight seconds. There is nothing else to do. Observe your breathing, right here and now.

Notice your physical sensations – the feel of your feet on the floor, the rise and fall of your chest. You rapidly realize a more peaceful state, changing the moment in a wonderful way.

Either one of these techniques will bring your focus into the present moment and ground you in peace. Isn't that where everything gets handled anyway? The present moment.

Practicing this each day develops the ability to access your inner peace automatically during a crisis or emergency situation. It's a grounding technique that can help you stay centered during the chaos.

Bonus Tip: The Power of the Pause

Before diving headfirst into working through an emergency, take a deep breath – a tiny pause. Composed action is better than a flurry of frantic movements. Assess the situation and then, like a Superhero with a plan, go forth and handle it!

With a little effort and these handy tools, you'll be navigating hospital chaos with the inner peace of a meditating monk (except way cooler, because you're a Nurse, which is basically a real-life Superhero).

Integrating Mindfulness into Daily Life

You don't have to be a meditation master to reap the benefits of mindfulness. There are many simple ways to incorporate mindfulness into your daily life. One of the easiest ways to practice mindfulness is through mindful eating.

Instead of mindlessly scarfing down your lunch, take a few moments to savor each bite. Pay attention to the flavors, textures, and aromas. Become aware of your body breathing in-between bites.

This mindful effort goes a long way in allowing the mind to calm and helps you to appreciate the simple pleasures in life.

Mindful walking is another great way to practice mindfulness. As you walk, focus on your breath and the sensations in your body. Notice the sights, sounds, and smells around you.

This can help you to feel more grounded and present. Remember, mindfulness is not about being perfect. It's about being present and accepting things as they are in the moment.

With a little practice, you can learn to cultivate mindfulness in your daily life and experience the many benefits it has to offer. This will be covered in a bit more detail in the remaining pages.

Meditation - It's Like Scrubs, But Way More Comfortable

Congratulations on taking a giant leap towards a calmer, more mindful you. High fives all around! But remember, this guide is just the beginning.

Think of meditation as the mechanism for accessing peace. Why keep going? Because learning to stabilize in peace doesn't happen overnight

Just like it takes time to master that tricky IV stick, mastering meditation takes practice. Don't get discouraged if you don't achieve instant inner peace.

The key is consistency. A few minutes of meditation each day can make a world of difference in your stress levels, focus, and overall well-being.

3 Tips to help you on your Meditation Journey

1. **Find Your Meditation Groove:** There's no "best" way for you to meditate. Experiment with different techniques (guided meditations, mindfulness exercises, focusing on your breath) and find what works best for you. Think of it like trying on different scrubs – some styles fit better than others!

2. **Short and Sweet is Still Super Sweet:** Don't have hours to dedicate to meditation? No sweat! Even a few minutes a day can be incredibly beneficial. Start small, with 2 to 5-minute sessions, and gradually increase the time as you become more comfortable.

3. **Be Kind to Yourself (Especially When Your Mind Wanders):** Our minds are naturally like curious puppies – always sniffing out distractions. Don't beat yourself up if

your focus strays during meditation. Simply acknowledge the wandering thought and gently bring your attention back to your breath. It's all part of the practice!

Remember: You are a badass nurse who has already conquered countless challenges. Meditation is just another skill to add to your Superhero arsenal.

So keep practicing, be patient with yourself, and enjoy the journey towards a calmer, more mindful you.

After all, a happy nurse is a healthy nurse, and a healthy nurse is a Superhero for their patients (and themself!).

P.S. If you have a bad day (and let's be honest, even Superheroes have those), don't abandon meditation altogether. Sometimes, those are the very days you need it most.

So grab your favorite comfy spot, take a few deep breaths, and hit that reset button. You've got this!

Chapter Six

The Nurse Whisperer's Toolkit

The Mind Meld: Nurse Edition

Ever felt like a human pinball, bouncing between patient rooms, doctors' orders, and the vending machine for your third cup of "pick me up"?

Welcome to the glamorous world of nursing! But fear not, weary warrior, for you possess a secret weapon: the power of the mind meld.

No, we're not talking about green-skinned aliens here. A nurse mind meld is the art of connecting with patients on a level deeper than small talk and bedside manners.

It's about becoming a human MRI, scanning for unspoken needs, hidden fears, and the occasional craving for chocolate milk.

Why bother with this stuff? Well, imagine being able to instantly decipher why your patient is eyeing the call button for the fifth time or why their "fine" suddenly means "I'm about to cry."

This telepathic connection doesn't just make you a super nurse; it transforms you into a patient whisperer, building trust and creating a healing environment that's more relaxing than a spa day.

So, how do you channel your inner Spock and master the mind meld? Here are a couple of tips to get you started:

Active Listening 101: Stop, drop, and really listen. We mean, really listen. Put down that chart, make eye contact, and let your patient know you're fully present. It's like giving your undivided attention a standing ovation.

Empathy Wear: Slip into your patient's shoes (or hospital gown). Imagine how it would feel to be on the receiving end of needles, beeping machines, and questionable hospital food. A little empathy goes a long way in making someone feel understood and cared for.

Mirroring and Validation: Sometimes the best medicine is a listening ear. Reflect back key points of what they've said to show you're paying attention.

For example: ("It sounds like you're feeling frustrated about your pain medication"). Validate their feelings, even if you can't fix everything. ("I understand why you'd be upset. Pain can be very difficult to manage").

Remember, a successful mind meld is more than just a cool party trick. It's about building relationships, providing comfort, and ultimately, delivering better care. So live long and... well, you know the rest.

Humor

Humor is an invaluable tool in a nurse's arsenal. It can be a powerful antidote to the often stressful and emotionally charged environment of healthcare.

Reduces Stress: Laughter is a natural stress reliever for both patients and nurses.

Builds Rapport: Humor can help create a relaxed and comfortable atmosphere, fostering trust between nurse and patient.

Distracts from Pain: A well-timed joke can divert a patient's attention from discomfort.

Enhances Communication: Humor can open up lines of communication and make difficult conversations easier.

Boosts Morale: A shared laugh can lift the spirits of both staff and patients.

A Humorous Example

Imagine a nurse caring for an elderly patient (or a child) who is a bit resistant to taking their medication. The nurse, with a twinkle in her eye, might say, "This pill is like a tiny Superhero, ready to fight off those pesky germs. Are you ready to unleash the

Superhero?" (some add a lame attempt at Superhero theme music) Dun dun dun! Pause for effect.

Yep, you'll probably see eyes rolling or even hear a non-pain related groan. This playful approach can often turn a dreaded task into a lighthearted moment, even if the patient simply laughs, or groans, at how silly you are. It's one more powerful tool to change the moment.

Important Note: While humor is a valuable tool, it's essential to use it appropriately and respectfully. Nurses must always be mindful of their patients' emotional state and cultural background. Humor should never be used to belittle or make fun of someone.

Bonus Tool: The Power of Positive Body Language

The impact of nonverbal communication is huge! Maintain open body language – uncrossed arms, good eye contact – to project warmth and approachability.

A genuine smile (even if it's under your mask) can go a long way in building rapport with patients and colleagues. Remember, becoming a Nurse Whisperer takes practice.

There will be bumps along the road (like that time you accidentally called Mr. Johnson " Mr. Smith" – oops!), but with these tools and a dash of compassion, you'll be navigating patient communication like a seasoned pro.

Before you know it, you'll be forming connections so strong; you'll swear you can practically hear your patients' thoughts (but hopefully not the ones about the hospital food!).

Starting Your Meditation Routine

Let's face it, fitting meditation into your already jam-packed nurse schedule can feel like trying to squeeze a beach vacation into your lunch break.

But fear not, warriors of the white coat! This guide will transform you from a meditation skeptic to a peace wielding Superhero.

Why Meditate consistently?

Daily meditation is like giving your brain a spa day. It reduces stress, improves focus, and can even help you sleep better (which, let's be honest, is a nurse's dream).

Practicing even short meditations each day creates momentum and that momentum turns into a beautiful balance of work and peace. A calm and centered nurse is really a Superhero for their patients!

Making Meditation a Habit

Here are a few ways to motivate, reward, inspire and help you make meditation a daily routine.

1. **Reward Yourself Silly:** (But With Healthy Options!) We all have motivators. Chocolate for quiet contemplation? Totally understandable. But for a more well-rounded approach, consider post-meditation rewards like fruit or a favorite treat.

2. **Buddy Up:** (But Not Literally on Your Meditation Mat) Find a friend or colleague to join you on your meditation journey. The accountability can be a game-changer, plus, sharing the struggle (and the post-meditation non-chocolate reward) can be a bonding experience.

3. **The "Shower Om":** Who says meditation requires fancy cushions and incense (although, those can be nice too)? Turn your daily shower into a mini-meditation session.

   Focus on the feeling of the water on your skin, the sound of the running water, and simply be present in the moment. Feel the water and be mindful of your breathing. It's a great way to wash away stress.

4. **The "Charting Zen" Technique:** Feeling overwhelmed by documentation? Add in some mindful breathing while you chart! As you click or write a few words, take a slow, deep breath in. As you finish the note, exhale slowly. It's a sneaky way to incorporate mindfulness into your workday and no one will even know you're doing it.

Living Your Meditations

Transforming the Mundane into the Mindful

Taking your meditation practice beyond the cushion and into daily life is where the real magic happens.

By weaving mindful moments into everyday tasks, you cultivate a sense of calm and awareness that transcends the formal meditation session. Here are several examples to inspire you:

The Mindful Meal

The Situation: You're starving after a long shift and practically inhale your dinner.

The Living Meditation: Before taking a bite, pause for a moment. Silently acknowledge your hunger and appreciate the food in front of you. Take a few slow breaths, noticing the aroma and visual appeal of your meal. Slowly move to take your first bite.

As you eat, chew slowly, savoring each flavor and texture. You can observe breathing in-between each bite and each movement of the fork or spoon.

This mindful approach can be practiced at breakfast, lunch or dinner and transforms a rushed meal into a nourishing and grounding experience.

The Mindful Shower

The Situation: You're exhausted and just want to scrub away the day's stress in the shower.

The Living Meditation: Instead of letting your mind be on autopilot, turn your shower into a mini-meditation.

Feel the water cascading down your body, noticing the temperature and sensation on your skin.

Focus on your breath, allowing steam to gently cleanse your mind as well. Allow the water to wash over you while you observe your breathing. This mindful awareness transforms a routine chore into a rejuvenating experience.

The Mindful Commute

The Situation: Stuck in traffic, frustration mounts as the minutes tick by.

The Living Meditation: Instead of fuming or rushing, transform your commute into a meditation on patience.

Before leaving, take a few seconds to focus on yo ur breath, acknowledging the urge to rush but choosing to accept the situation and drive safely. Take a slow deep breath in and out, then begin your trip.

If you forgot to practice before you left and find yourself stuck in traffic, take a minute (with your eyes open) to become aware of your breathing while you wait for the traffic to move. This will help to remove the anxiety and impatience.

In fact, you may even notice more of the sights and sounds you usually miss on autopilot. This mindful approach helps you arrive at your destination feeling calmer and more centered.

You'll find that you really do have the power to change the way a situation is experienced. It happens because you chose to observe breath and dwell in peace.

The Mindful Phone Call

The Situation: You're catching up with a friend or family member, but your mind is already racing with the next response or the next thing on your to-do list.

The Living Meditation: Make a conscious effort to be fully present during the conversation. Bring your awareness to your breathing and settle into peace.

Listen attentively, focusing on the words being spoken and the emotions conveyed. Don't rush to reply, listen more. Many times you'll be able to understand the intent behind the words, which can tell you a lot. Know this, a person can tell when you're genuinely listening.

The next thing is very important. Take a deep breath before responding. This allows your thoughts to settle and your response to be clear and appropriate.

This mindful approach fosters deeper and more meaningful interactions. Practicing this technique will enhance communication with family, friends, colleagues, a spouse or children.

The Mindful Fold

(Laundry Time!)

The Situation: You're facing a mountain of laundry after a long week and feeling overwhelmed by the never-ending chore.

The Living Meditation: Instead of dreading the task, transform laundry folding into a mindful meditation.

Pick up each item, feeling the texture and warmth of the fabric. Focus on the simple act of folding, noticing the repetitive movements of your arms.

Notice your body breathing while you make each fold.

If your mind wanders, gently bring your attention back to the present moment and the task at hand. Simply become aware of your breathing while folding.

You can even time your breaths with each fold. Try it! This mindful approach can transform a mundane chore into a surprisingly peaceful experience.

While you start out slow and methodical, you may find that the chore seems to fly right by – done before you know it.

Remember, these are just a few examples. The possibilities for living meditations are endless. The key is to bring your awareness to the present moment and to your breath, no matter the activity.

By weaving mindfulness into the fabric of your daily life, you create a sense of calm and peace that extends far beyond the meditation cushion.

Remember: Consistency is key! Start with just a few minutes of meditation a day, and gradually increase the time as you become more comfortable.

OK...we have covered several techniques, their benefits and ways to use them. By now, you may have found a technique you're willing to try. That's fantastic, but don't worry if you haven't.

This book is full of techniques and in the following pages; you're bound to find a technique that will work for you. They are all based in the breath, something you constantly have access to.

When you're ready, give it a try, but don't expect anything. Just try it, without expectations. Don't get discouraged if your mind wanders – it's natural! Just gently bring your attention back to your breath.

Before you know it, meditation will become a natural part of your day, leaving you feeling more centered, focused, and ready to conquer whatever the nursing gods throw your way (and maybe even resist the urge to hoard all the good snacks in the break room – but we can't promise miracles!).

The Nurse Tribe: You're Not Alone

Nursing can be tough at times. But fear not, you are not alone on this journey. There's a whole tribe of nurses out there seeking solace and serenity, and guess what?

They're probably online, sharing war stories (the funny kind, we hope) and tips for staying sane... or at least sane-ish.

It is very important to make the distinction between support and inspiration verses wallowing in misery with others. Make sure that the group you participate with makes a positive impact on your life.

Why Join the Nurse Tribe?

Meditation can feel pretty personal, but let's be honest, sometimes you just need a good laugh with people who understand the specific brand of crazy that is the nursing life. Online communities offer a supportive space to share your journey with others on a similar path.

Share your meditation wins (and fails – we've all been there): Did you finally achieve inner peace while charting? Or did your mind wander off to plan your dream vacation house on a deserted island? These online groups can be a good space to share your experiences.

Find encouragement and motivation: Feeling discouraged? The nurse tribe has your back! They'll offer words of encouragement and help you get back on track with your meditation practice.

Discover new meditation resources: These online communities are a treasure trove of meditation apps, guided meditations, and mindfulness tips specifically tailored to nurses.

Where to Find Your Nurse Tribe

The internet is a vast and wonderful place, but here are a few suggestions to get you started. Important: Make sure to read the group descriptions and join one that resonates with you.

Facebook Groups: There are numerous Facebook groups dedicated to mindful nurses. Search for terms like "mindful nurses," "nurse meditation," or "nurse self-care."

Online Forums: Many nursing websites and online forums have sections dedicated to meditation and stress management. These can be a great way to connect with nurses from all over the world.

Social Media: Follow hashtags like #mindfulnurse or #nurseswhomeditate on platforms like Instagram or Twitter. You'll find a wealth of inspirational content and connect with other mindful nurses.

Remember: The key is to find a community that feels like a good fit. Don't be afraid to explore different groups and see where you feel most welcome.

So, silence those inner gremlins, grab your metaphorical meditation mat (or favorite comfy chair), and join the nurse tribe!

You'll be surprised at the support, humor, and sense of camaraderie you'll find on your journey to mindfulness.

And hey, if a meditation group isn't your cup of tea (or coffee, as the case may be), that's okay too! The important thing is to find healthy ways to de-stress and recharge.

Mindfulness in leadership

So, you're a nurse leader. You're juggling schedules, dealing with staffing shortages, and probably fielding more questions than a customer service hotline.

Sounds stressful, right? Well, that's where meditation comes in. Think of it as your personal "pause button" in a world that's always on fast forward.

Why is it important for leaders?

Stress Relief: Let's face it, nursing can be a challenge, especially as a leader or manager. Meditation helps you stay calm, cool, and collected, even when you're dealing with a patient who's got more demands than a diva.

Improved Focus: Imagine trying to focus on a patient's care plan while your phone is buzzing with texts and your coworker is asking you about their PTO.

Meditation helps you tune out the noise, prioritize and concentrate on what matters. This is important for good leadership.

Enhanced Decision-Making: When you're stressed, it's easy to make rash decisions. Meditation helps you approach problems with a clear head, so you can make the best choices for your patients and your team.

It is true that the best teachers are those who teach by example. As a Nurse Leader who meditates, you will set an example for others simply by the way you live your life.

You don't have to teach meditation to teach those around you. They will see its effects on you and they will experience the peace you bring to the floor.

You may find that people listen to you more because you are speaking less. You are speaking less because you are listening more. From a place of peace, your speech, your planning and action become more effective.

The Connection between Mindfulness and Compassion

Ever felt like you were running on fumes? As a nurse, you're constantly juggling patients, families, and your own personal life.

It's easy to get caught up in the job mechanics and forget about the human being behind the diagnosis. That's where mindfulness comes in.

Mindfulness is really like a Superpower for nurses. It's the ability to be fully present in the moment, without judgment.

When you're mindful, you're more attuned to your patients' emotions, their pain, and their fears.

From a calm center, you understand what you're experiencing is a temporary version of that person in pain. For that reason, you're less likely to get caught up in the drama of the situation and more likely to offer genuine compassion.

Imagine you're caring for a patient who's just received a devastating diagnosis. Instead of rushing through the conversation, you take a moment to breathe deeply and connect with the patient on a human level.

You listen attentively to their concerns, validate their feelings, and offer comfort. That's the power of mindfulness.

It is important to note that when you are anchored in peace, you can help others process emotions and are much less likely to be swept away by them yourself. You become a lighthouse of calm in their storm.

The ability to do this is a natural side effect (Superhero power) of a consistent meditation practice – yes, even a short one.

Mindfulness for Nurses in Specific Specialties

There is no doubt that practicing meditation will enhance the career of any nurse and help bring balance to the human experience.

However, mindfulness can be particularly helpful for nurses in certain specialties. For example, emergency room nurses often deal with high-stress situations.

If you're an **E.R. Nurse,** breath based mindfulness techniques, like those found throughout this book, can help you stay calm and focused, even in the midst of chaos. It can also help you to regulate your emotions (heart strings) and avoid burnout.

Short, "go to" mindfulness techniques can quickly transform an experience from "Things are really crazy!" into the experience of "I am the peace in this crazy!"

It changes the moment. You become centered, the witness of what is needed now and with that clarity, you act.

Pediatric nurses, on the other hand, often work with young patients who may be even more scared or anxious. Mindfulness can help you to connect with children on a deeper level and offer comfort and support.

It can also help you to be more patient and understanding. This can be a real Superhero power when dealing with a frightened child or one with special needs.

The child will literally "feel" your peace. They may not know why they like being around you, or why they feel better when you're around, but you will know. From a place of peace you share a smile or a laugh (which is the sound of a smile).

The strength of your peace is developed through meditation and your ability to share it flows through presence, guided by intellect and the heart. Simply put, children are innocent and live the best they know how.

You bring peace to their scary situation. They remember the Nurse that made all the difference in the world during their stay, and if they don't, you can bet the parents will.

When kids are scared, they look for comfort and besides the parents, there is nothing more comforting than a Superhero Nurse with the power of peace.

Chapter Seven

The Nurse's Reference to Guided Meditations

Some things to remember:

There are many forms of meditation, structured, posture based, etc. However, for the techniques suggested in this book, all you'll need is butt and breath. Sit on your "butt" comfortably, relaxed and in a position that's easy to breath.

Don't worry about sitting stiff or a certain way. Sit comfortably and quietly. Your body should be relaxed and your inner gaze focused on the breathing.

If your mind wanders, don't panic! Just gently bring your attention back to the present moment – to your breath.

Find your groove, a meditation practice (short or long) that works for you. Go ahead, grab your meditation mat (or a comfy chair) and try it! Now let's look at a way to find time to be mindful at work, even when there seems to be none.

Finding A Way

Often, the best we can do is take a quick break. We go to the bathroom, stretch our legs with a short walk or go get a drink.

Usually, you can find a quiet spot to catch your breath and become mindful of it, at least for a couple of minutes.

If you find it difficult to find any place with 2 minutes of quiet, fear not, all is not lost. There is a distance, a space between you and the patient's room. You go to their room many times a day and night. That means you have that short walk over and over.

Prepare your mind for the walk by reviewing what you need to do for your patient when you arrive. Once done, let it go and start the walk.

No one will know what you're doing, except you! Become mindful of your breathing during the walk. Don't mentally go into the room until you arrive.

Keep your focus on your breath. Become aware of your breathing as you walk. Maintain this until you arrive at the door, then take one deep breath and enter the room upon exhaling.

You will find that even this short walk can add to your meditation routine and make a huge difference in maintaining peace.

You don't space out or become forgetful. You walk mindfully, aware of your breathing until you arrive. Then, anchored in peace, you enter the room.

This small effort will help you reduce stress, gain clarity and keep you on the peaceful side of life as a nurse.

We have covered some ways that meditation can help you with the challenges of being a nurse and provided you with a few techniques to get you started.

There are endless possibilities for creating your own short, helpful meditations to combat everyday nursing challenges. Our hope is that you will try one out and see for yourself. If you give it an honest try, you won't be disappointed.

While there is no doubt that meditation can help you navigate the stressful waters of work, it's important to leave work at work, when you get home.

Letting go of the job when you're not there

This next line may be the most important one in this whole book. *You are not a Nurse. Being a Nurse is just the job you do.*

Underneath the "Nurse" is a living breathing human. One with a body that needs care and a mind that needs downtime.

So many Nurses forget that and become lost in the job and the stress. It's easy to do and there are many contributing factors.

The most significant reason for becoming lost in the stress of the job is that you have identified yourself with your job. You feel like the job is you. If the job is going well, you feel good. If the job is going bad, you feel bad.

When you step back into your peace, the sway of good and bad has less pull. YOU can still experience a peaceful day, regardless of the circumstance (tough or easy).

The techniques you find here will help you to find your way out of the turmoil of misidentification and into peace.

While we have discussed some techniques that address the "before, during and after a shift" meditations, it's time now to discuss a few more techniques that you can practice any time you are at home and have a little more time.

These techniques are specifically to help you realize the peace **you are** underneath the person you imagine as "Nurse".

Unmasking the Superhero Within

Why Nurses Need Home Meditation

Nurses, our modern-day Superheroes, often find themselves caught in a whirlwind of chaos and stress.

With long hours, demanding patients, and a constant barrage of information, it's no wonder that many nurses feel overwhelmed and exhausted.

While mindfulness techniques like deep breathing and short meditations can be helpful during work hours, it's equally important to find ways to de-stress and calm the mind at home.

Imagine you're a Superhero who's just fought off a horde of Supervillains. You're exhausted, but you still have to save the world tomorrow.

What do you do? You don't just grab a coffee and dive back into the action. You find a quiet spot, relax, and recharge.

Home meditation is like your secret Superhero hideout, a place where you can unwind, rejuvenate, and connect with your inner power of peace. By dedicating a few minutes each day to meditation, nurses can:

Reduce stress and anxiety: Instead of feeling like you're about to explode or lose it, meditation can help you calm down and feel more relaxed.

Improve sleep quality: Imagine trying to function at work on little to no sleep. It's tough, right? Meditation can help you sleep better so you can be a Superhero every day.

Enhance emotional resilience: Nurses often witness suffering and trauma, which can be like battling a never-ending villain. Meditation can help you develop a Superhero-level resilience.

Boost creativity and problem-solving skills: When you're stressed, it's like trying to solve a puzzle with your hands tied behind your back. Meditation can pave the way for problem solving by helping you think more clearly and creatively.

Cultivate self-awareness and compassion: By turning inward and observing your thoughts and feelings, you can become a more compassionate and understanding Superhero.

Meditations for Home

The following 8 meditations are designed to help nurses unwind, relax, and recharge at home. There are four 15 minute meditations and four 30-60 minute meditations.

Remember, the goal is not to achieve perfection, but simply to find a practice that works for you. A simple home practice combined with the short techniques at work make for a wonderful combination, one that will change the way you experience your life.

The peace, stillness and grace that you are, is waiting to be experienced. So let's put on the fuzzy socks and unleash your inner Superhero with these home meditation techniques!

15 Minute Meditations

1. The Breath of Awareness

Instructions:

Sit comfortably with your spine straight.

Close your eyes gently.

Bring your attention to your breath. Observe the natural rhythm of your inhales and exhales.

As you breathe, notice the sensations in your body. The friction of air moving past your nostrils or even the temperature difference of the air coming in verses the air moving out.

When your mind wanders, gently bring it back to your breath. Simply dwell in the background of silence. Become the observer, the witness of your body breathing.

Benefits: This meditation helps to seat your perception in awareness. It anchors the mind in the present moment, reducing anxiety and promoting a sense of calm.

2. The Heart Meditation

Instructions:

Sit comfortably with your spine straight.

Place your hands over your heart.

Visualize light radiating from your hands, filling your heart with the warm glow of peace and love.

As you calmly breathe in and out, feel the love expanding throughout your body. As this light continues to fill the body, the mind settles and activity fades into the pure presence of light.

Benefits: This meditation helps to open the heart, fostering compassion, forgiveness, and a sense of connection with others.

Many notice that even after you relax your gaze and no longer imagine the light within, you still feel it. It remains ever present as a beacon of peace.

3. The Mantra Meditation

Instructions:

Choose a mantra (two sacred words) that resonate with you. Choose words that mean something to you such as "Om Shanti" (Peace), "I Am" or "God Is". The focus is placed on each word as you breathe in and out.

The first word is internally chanted (as a thought) on the inhale and the second word on the exhale.

If you prefer, many speak the Mantra or words aloud, softly and at the beginning of each inhale and exhale.

Some prefer to stretch each word out during the breath in and again on the out breath. Experiment and find out what works for you.

Sit comfortably with your spine straight and relaxed. Repeat the mantra silently or aloud, focusing on the sound and vibration. Give it a try and you will quickly know which is right for you.

Allow the mantra to fill your mind and heart with peace and tranquility. Keep the focus on the words as you breathe.

If your attention wonders, just bring it back to the mantra. When you're ready, stop the mantra. Just sit quietly, aware of your body breathing. Go for it!

Benefits: Mantra meditation helps to quiet the mind, reduce stress, and promote a sense of inner peace. This one is very helpful for those with active or busy minds.

4. The Gratitude Meditation

Instructions:

Sit comfortably with your spine relaxed and relatively straight.

Close your eyes and take a few deep breaths.

Begin to recall things you are grateful for in your life. Nature, a friend, a family member, a pet, a job, food, it can be anything!

Focus on the feelings of gratitude that arise within you. Notice the feelings as they come and go, just like your breath.

Uninvolved, you observe the memories and the feelings of gratitude. You remain the silent witness of them all, allowing each one to come and go.

Benefits: Gratitude meditation helps to shift your focus towards the positive aspects of your life, promoting happiness and contentment.

Bonus: The following is an example of how to turn the act of eating a piece of candy (or just about anything) into a wonderful meditation.

The Mindful Gummy Bear

Sometimes, a little indulgence can be a great stress reliever. This meditation combines mindfulness with a sweet treat (because nurses deserve both!).

Acquire a piece of your favorite soft candy; in this case we are using a Gummy Bear for our example. In the event you have a hard piece of candy, you can still adapt this act of mindfulness to it.

Instructions:

1. **Unwrap the Gummy:** Slowly open the bag and remove a gummy bear, savoring the sound and sensation. As you do, take a deep breath in and out, focusing on the present moment.

2. **Examine the Gummy (Observe):** Hold the gummy bear up to the light, observing its color, shape, and texture. Appreciate the simple beauty of this tiny treat.

3. **Savor the Flavor (Mindful Bite):** Take a small bite of the gummy bear. Notice the taste and texture, chewing slowly and mindfully.

4. **The Zen Chew:** With each chew, feel your body relax and your stress melt away. Mindful of your breath, enjoy the simple pleasure of the moment. By doing this, you create a space for peace to be experienced; a peace that remains long after the candy is gone.

These meditations are wonderful ways to practice mindfulness in a short amount of time. However, if you wish to extend your practice and have 30 minutes to an hour, here are 4 more meditations for those days when you have a bit longer to spend meditating

30 to 60 Minute Meditations

Preparation Tips for Longer Meditations

Find a Quiet Space: Choose a peaceful environment free from distractions and interruptions if possible.

Comfortable Posture: Sit upright with your spine comfortably straight and relaxed.

Mindfulness of Breath: Pay attention to your natural breathing rhythm. It doesn't matter if your focal point is the chest, stomach, mouth or the tip of the nose. Do what works for you.

Gentle Focus: Avoid straining your mind. Let thoughts come and go without judgment. Dwell as the silent background, aware of passing thoughts, but remaining uninvolved. By withdrawing attention from the activity of thought, mind calms and peace asserts itself.

1. Breath Observation Meditation

Instructions:

Establish a Comfortable Posture: Sit upright with your spine straight but relaxed.

Focus on your Breath: Observe your natural breathing rhythm as your body settles.

Witness the Breath: Follow the breath all the way in and all the way out. Notice the rise and fall of your chest or abdomen.

Shift Perception: Recognize yourself as the observer of the body breathing, not involved, just observing. The body knows how to breathe and it will. Simply observe the body breathing.

Let go of any thoughts of past or future and simply experience the present moment. Remain aware of the body breathing. When you're ready, relax your inner gaze and end the meditation with a deep relaxing breath.

Benefits: This meditation helps to cultivate mindfulness, reduce anxiety, and improve concentration. It is also considered one of the simplest and most powerful practices.

2. The Inner Garden Meditation

Instructions:

Establish a Comfortable Posture: Sit upright with your spine straight but relaxed.

Focus on the Breath: Observe your breath as you settle into a natural and relaxed breathing rhythm. Let your body settle as you follow the air all the way in and out of your body.

Visualize: Imagine your mind as a garden. This spacious garden can produce both beautiful flowers (positive thoughts) and big weeds (negative thoughts). The current condition of your garden doesn't matter. It's a starting place.

Tend to the Garden: It's time to water the flowers of peace, while removing weeds of worry and fear. Mind is the garden and you're simply caring for it by tending to it.

By observing this garden (mind) in meditation, you'll find yourself able to "catch a thought"; and have the ability to pluck a negative thought (weed) and replace it by planting a positive thought (flower) in your garden.

Address one thought at a time. If it's negative, pluck it and let it go. If it's positive, water it by lingering on it. This is what is meant by "Tending to your garden".

One example of this visualization is of a small ball of light (a positive thought) turning into a flower. When a weed (negative thought) is discovered, it's removed and vanishes in a puff of smoke that fades away.

You have cut it from the garden by withdrawing your attention from it. In fact, because you are tending to the garden (observing thought), YOU get to say which thought stays in the peaceful garden and which goes. YOU are the gardener.

This happens because you are sitting in silence and observing the minds activity – thought. Eventually, you'll find your heart smiling when you observe your garden and it's overflowing with the flowers of peace.

When you're ready, take a deep breath and allow the garden to be done for now. Put the gardening tools away and relax.

This meditation may take some time to sort out in your imagination, but it can be a very beautiful and valuable meditation. It will foster a more positive outlook and is great for those who consider themselves imaginative or visual.

Benefits: This meditation helps to cultivate inner peace, reduce anxiety, develop mindful actions and promote self-awareness.

This practice focuses on replacing negative thoughts with positive; which is really great for staying out of the dumps.

3. The Story of Your Life Meditation

Instructions:

Establish a Comfortable Posture: Sit upright with your spine straight but relaxed.

Focus on Breath: Observe your body's natural breathing rhythm. Take some time to let everything settle, your body, your breath and your mind.

Visualize Your Life: Imagine your life as a story unfolding before you. Start from whatever age you like, a child, teen, adult, it doesn't matter. Mentally begin to move forward through the memories of your life. Observe each one as they pass, but do not linger.

Keep moving slowly toward the present. Let go of any judgment and simply observe the story without attachment – like watching a movie.

Shift Perception: Recognize yourself as the silent witness of this whole story, not as the main character. In this action, you are seating your perception in the awareness of the story, not in being the character. This takes a bit of effort, a mental action of sorts.

Eventually, you'll realize yourself as the one that never changes throughout the story – the Witness. You were always there, as the observer, just as you are right now. Everything else you experience simply comes and goes, just like the breath.

Benefits: This meditation helps to gain perspective on life's challenges and cultivate a sense of detachment. Action is still performed; the story goes on, but with less entanglement and a great deal more peace.

4. The Divine Light Meditation

This meditation uses the religious name for the divine as you know it. While you may use any name you like, we will use the name "God" for this example.

Instructions:

Establish a Comfortable Posture: Sit upright with your spine straight but relaxed. This meditation is for those who practice a religion and prefer to have a Divine power (Gods grace) as a part of their meditation.

Focus on Breath: Observe your natural breathing rhythm. Say a personal prayer thanking God for his grace (presence) in your meditation.

Visualize Divine Light: Imagine yourself surrounded by a radiant, golden light. Know that the radiant light surrounding you is divine grace, the presence of God.

Now imagine all the light of God's grace being absorbed into your body, into every cell.

Remain aware of the body breathing until the light is fully absorbed. Recognize yourself as a vessel for divine light. Bring your attention to your breathing as the light completely fills you.

Realize that you are the stillness, aware of the body breathing. You are the witness, aware of this body full of light. With a slow deep breath, relax your gaze and sit quietly in grace.

Benefits: This meditation helps to cultivate a sense of peace, love, and connection with a higher power. It's a great practice for taking a deep dive into the divine.

Additional Meditative Practices

These instructions are easy to remember and simple to carry out. As always, insure that you are safe. Become mindful of your breathing while you do any of the following:

Take a walk in nature. A slow mindful walk in the wilderness can reconnect you with the peace in your heart. Turn your ringer off and spend some time walking among the trees.

Being out in nature is one of the most healing activities on the planet. Everything in nature becomes a teacher of peace, if you listen.

Folding laundry or Washing dishes. These are two great ways to practice mindfulness. They both provide a wonderful, breath based mechanism for entering the present moment.

They each give you the opportunity to add a meditative moment to your day by turning a chore into an act of mindfulness.

When folding laundry, simply be mindful of your body breathing while you do it. With each movement, feel the warmth and texture of the item you're folding. Take your time with each fold and each breath.

When doing the dishes, remain aware of your breathing as the flow of the water washes over your hands. Notice the temperature of the water and the texture of the dish. By remembering your breath, you can turn the mundane into an act of mindfulness.

Parents with Children. Every time your child calls your name, mom, dad, etc, take a slow deep breath and follow that air all the way in and out. Afterwards, attend to the child from a place of peace. (Yes, it actually works)

Crafting or Cooking. Either of these activities offers a chance to be mindful while you do them. Whether its chopping ingredients or crafting a quilt, remaining aware of your breath can turn each movement into a mindful one. Try it!

Remember, it doesn't matter how often you become mindful or how long you meditate. The fact that you ARE meditating, matters most. Every little bit of time you spend observing your breath (even 30 seconds) creates momentum.

Meditation may still seem new or silly or even intimidating, but all you have to do is give it an honest try and you will wonder why you waited so long. Your peace is the real Superpower. Meditation is the practice by which you access it. This book helps you with that practice.

Plain and simple, it works. Now go and be that person you want to be, the best version of yourself.

Ignore the thought "I can't meditate" and embrace the idea of "I do meditate". Start now. Take two minutes. Be the mindful Nurse that Meditates often and live your peace!

A Final note

For those of you who use this information and find out for yourself that it really works, well done! To those of you who use these techniques to find peace in the middle of chaos, you rock!

However, for those of you who have developed a consistent practice and are looking to dive a bit deeper into self-inquiry, we'd like to offer the following:

After mastering the breath, the next focus is on the mind, specifically the activity of thought. The mind, sometimes described as the "chitta" in Sanskrit, is often seen as a turbulent ocean of thoughts and emotions. When these calm, the true nature of the Self can be revealed.

Here's a breakdown of the process:

Observation of Thoughts: Start by simply observing your thoughts without judgment. Notice their patterns, their intensity, and their effects on your emotions. Don't engage, just witness.

Dissociation: Gradually, learn to dissociate yourself from your thoughts. Recognize that you are not your thoughts, but rather the observer of them.

Witnessing Consciousness: As you become more adept at observing your thoughts, you'll begin to notice a deeper level of consciousness - the witness.

This witnessing awareness is the true Self, the unchanging, eternal aspect of your being. The solid still peace within you.

Key points to remember:

Non-attachment: The goal is not to eliminate thoughts but to observe them without attachment.

Witnessing: The key to self-realization is to identify yourself as the awareness, which is aware of your thoughts and experiences.

The bottom line is, meditation works for Nurses. By cultivating the ability to access your own inner stillness, you'll gradually move closer to the ultimate goal of being anchored in an unshakable (Superhero level) peace. Start simple, start now and change your life.

The End